Visiting Biblical Saints in Heaven: Book 2

Matthew Robert Payne

Published by RWG Publishing, 2022.

Table of Contents

Visiting Biblical Saints in Heaven:
Book 2
Matthew Robert Payne

DEDICATION

This book is written for the spiritually hungry people out there who are so desperate for more of Jesus they will even travel with an author to Heaven to hear Biblical saints speak to them. May this book bless you. The saints in this book want to hear from you so be sure to write a review on Amazon and tell them which of them were your favorites in this interview book series.

Introduction

Welcome to my second book, *Visiting Biblical Saints in Heaven: Book 2*. If you missed the first one, be sure to download it now on Amazon because the saints in this book often refer back to what the previous ones said. In this book we explore the mansions of nine biblical saints as they answer three questions that shed light on their adventures in Heaven, what they like about Heaven, and what they want us to do with our time left on earth.

You may read these books and have an urge to start running after saints, desperately wanting to meet them. But I can assure you, you'll only meet true saints—and you'll only develop good relationships with them—if you first develop a great relationship with Jesus. Jesus won't allow you to start communicating with saints unless you've built significant rapport with Him first. Jesus is the center, and He should be *your* center. He should be the person that you worship, the person that you follow, and the person that you strive to emulate in everything you do.

With that warning fully established, journey with me to Heaven and hear of all its wonders.

Visiting Rahab in Heaven

This chapter begins with what I can see in Rahab's house in Heaven. First, I see her kitchen. There is a walk-in fridge that allows you to stroll through rows of cold meats, pineapples, and cherry tomatoes. There are shelves of different fruits and vegetables, including apples, oranges, pears, and bananas. I didn't expect to find bananas sitting in the fridge, but there they are.

Now, we're backing out of the fridge and into a walk-in pantry stacked with different groceries. Coming out of the pantry, there's a flat bench, nearly 10 feet long. It has a couple bench top stoves in the middle of it, and ovens on the wall behind it. It has extendable parts to it as well, allowing it to be stretched upwards at the end of the bench to make room for more workers.

Rahab's home has a 20-seat table in the dining room, with a picture of Jesus feeding the 5,000 hanging on the wall. There's also a very large picture of Jesus and His disciples handing out bread that seems to suit Rahab's characteristics and personality quite well. For those of you who've read my book, *Great Cloud of Witnesses Speak[1]*, you would know what Rahab does in Heaven. But for those of you who don't know yet, sit tight because we'll get to that part next.

The dining room table doesn't have revolving pictures embedded in it like the Apostle Peter's, but it does have images on the table, and various pictures of Rahab's former life. And she's very pretty, actually. There are images of her life on earth. One of them is from the time when she lived in Jericho, but the rest are with the tribes of Israel and her several roles and jobs with them. Now, on to the first question.

"What do you do in Heaven?"

Rahab answers, "I'm a chef in Heaven, Matthew. I run a couple of restaurants—three to be exact. I manage my time between each of them, six days a week. You can imagine that we don't have earthly time in

---

1.   https://www.amazon.com/dp/B07H3BWPGC

Heaven. We close on the sabbath, but other restaurants here operate on different schedules. For example, on the day my restaurant is closed, other restaurants remain open. To clarify—we don't have a formal Sabbath here in Heaven. I just work six days a week, so I like to refer to it as my own personal sabbath.

I really enjoy my work. I've taken the time to study in these past 2,000 years, and I've mastered every cuisine out there. I've learned how to cook Indian curries, Singapore noodles, Thai curries, and Thai dishes. My restaurants are filled with lengthy menus, all of which have a variety of meals to offer. I enjoy cooking for others.

I spend an amazing amount of time in my restaurants talking to the customers outside the kitchen. I'm very sociable and people love to meet me. I've got a balance of about 60/40 when it comes to returning customers and new customers. 60% of my customers are returning customers, and 40% are new each week, each day. The 40% are surprised that I come out of the kitchen and speak to them, and the 60% are regulars who are used to the way I operate. They love my company, and I love them. I've been told I'm like family to many of them, and that's because I spend quite a bit of my time getting to know about their life, and helping them grow in the things of the Lord.

I have chefs and waiters in my restaurant who serve and bring the food out. I have staff that are happy to work here. In terms of hierarchal operations, I have a second in charge—or a head chef—in each restaurant. They learn to speak to the customers too, so I'm not the only one who engages in this way. Every chef who is in charge of each of the restaurants spends his time on the floor, meaning speaking to customers.

I'm a female chef, and all my head chefs are men. However, I do have subsidiary chefs coming up and advancing in my restaurants that are women as well. I've found as professional chefs, men are very diligent in the kitchen, and they contribute greatly to the success of all my restaurants.

I enjoy cooking. I enjoy the feeling it brings to others, and the feelings it brings to myself. It's good to talk to a person and get their feedback when they've eaten a dish of yours. It's good to talk to them while they're eating the dish that you prepared.

We revolve the menus in each of my restaurants. One of my restaurants has the best dishes out of all three. This restaurant is called "The Best of Rahab", and it offers dishes that are customer favorites. Customers are given the opportunity to vote on dishes and provide feedback, which then helps us determine the dishes that should be placed on our "favorites" menu. These dishes are then shared and circulated in the restaurant.

Heaven has a lot of opportunity for feedback built into it. You can be voted the number one restaurant in Heaven. You can be voted the best cuisine in Heaven. Your individual dishes can be voted the best spaghetti Bolognese in Heaven. Your chefs can be voted the best chefs in Heaven. There are competitions and feedback on everything that we do in Heaven, keeping us sharp, motivated, and determined. We put an emphasis on doing our best and presenting the best meal that we can each time. Every meal that comes up is a part of perfection. We don't concentrate much on the rewards we receive from the customers and their votes, but it is worth mentioning that my restaurants have won "best restaurant" from time to time. The chefs have won "best chefs", our individual dishes have won "best cuisine", and our dishes have one "best meal".

Competitions aren't everything in Heaven, but they keep things exciting and novel. One of the chefs could put a different ingredient in one of the dishes because he's tried it out on himself and he thinks it's nice. Then you may be surprised that customers vote that dish "the best dish of the restaurant". That's when you know you're onto something good.

I like to keep people well-fed and happy. You can be sure when you come to Heaven that there's going to be enough food for everyone. You won't just come to my restaurants; you'll try many restaurants. There are restaurants dedicated to one cuisine only, like a Singapore restaurant, a Chinese restaurant, an Indian restaurant, or an Italian restaurant. We have multi-ethnic cuisines in our restaurants, but that's the way we like to cater to people, giving them a variety of foods to choose from at all times."

"What do you like about Heaven?"

"At the risk of sounding repetitive with the saints you've interviewed in Book 1, I must say that my favorite thing about Heaven is the people. I enjoy talking to people and spending time with them. Everyone in Heaven is on their own personal and spiritual journey. Everyone in Heaven is growing, and I like to learn about that growth. I like to converse with people and find out what they're up to, and how they're progressing.

I've got a deep spiritual faith and intimate walk with Jesus, and God the Father. I didn't have a good father when I was growing up. And so, I relate more to God. I spend a lot of time in God's presence and with Him individually. He's a real Father to me, and I really enjoy His presence. I enjoy speaking to Him one-on-one. I enjoy the worship in Heaven each earthly week. On those days of worship when the competition winners play their worship songs in the throne room, I attend those events and I really enjoy them.

Everyone gets a chance to meet the Father and sit next to Him or on His lap and talk to Him about anything and everything. He's been really good to me. He's brought out my strengths. I meet with Jesus once a week as everyone does, and everyone grows and receives assignments from Jesus. But most days, I pop in and spend some time with the Father. It's a real honor to be loved by our Father and to have God as our Father. It's a new dimension that you can walk in when you recognize God as your Father, and when He speaks and relates to you as a Father. I've established that relationship with Him where He looks out for me and encourages me. As a result, I've really grown in Heaven to become very close to God.

On that note, I move in the gift of prophecy. You may wonder whether prophecy exists in Heaven, and I want to assure you that it does. Anyone can speak on behalf of God. Often when I talk to a customer I'll just say, "God wants you to know this," followed by a prophetic statement. Many times the conversation ends in tears. The people are always really touched.

Matthew's prophecies normally come from Jesus. But when I prophesy, the messages come from the Father. He encourages people and gives them direction and comfort. So yes, prophecy does exist in Heaven. People have seen their future in Heaven, and you can watch your future unfold on a big screen in Heaven like a movie. But people tend to forget their future and what they're going to achieve. Prophecy really ignites that. So, I enjoy prophesying. I enjoy speaking to people and mixing with people. I enjoy spending time with the Father. I really like my interaction with Him, and it's a real blessing. I also enjoy Jesus.

Since Matthew is closest to Jesus, you'll find in this series of books that Jesus is mentioned more than the Father. But that's not because the Father isn't special to Matthew; it's just that Jesus is closer to him. Jesus is really is the center of Heaven, and He's dear to everyone. He really shines and stands out. The Father wouldn't have it any other way. He's given all authority to His Son. As a result, Jesus is the superstar of Heaven. It's natural that the saints talk about Him, but it's the God of Israel that have I come to love because the Israelis saved me and took me in from Jericho. I became a chef and cook in Israel, and I've been a cook ever since. It's much better than being a prostitute, I can tell you that.

Speaking to customers in my restaurant is similar to my life as a prostitute. I used to speak to my clients and have in-depth conversations with them. It's just the undressing and the sexual part that's different. Otherwise, I'm a real people person and people really enjoy me as well."

"What is your message for us?"

"It's really important for you to come to know Jesus. Whether it's Jesus or the Father, at least get to know one part of the Godhead. It's important for you to develop an intimacy with either God or Jesus. And as you come to know God more, the Scriptures will mean more to you.

Life will open up to you, and more opportunities will come your way. There'll be more times when you can praise God and be happy. I'm not saying that drawing close to the Father will instantaneously transform your life into a state of happiness. Some people really suffer and have terrible and hard lives, regardless of their rapport with God and Jesus. But being close to the Father will give you perspective and comfort. I encourage you all to learn how to hear from God. Matthew has a book on how to hear from God, and I encourage you all to learn how to hear God speak and how to hear Jesus speak by referring to that book as your guide.

So much benefit and reward can come to your life if you can hear God and Jesus speak. They add a certain dimension to your life that can't be offered otherwise. It's like if you were married and your wife never spoke to you. It would be a hard marriage to maintain. The same is true in the Christian life. Engaging in a one-sided relationship with God where you do not hear Him communicate or respond to you can create the basis of a faulty and weak relationship.

God has so much to offer. He has so much to share with you and so much to encourage you with. He doesn't just speak through prophets. He speaks personally and can encourage you in your daily life. He has a deep-rooted interest in you. I encourage you to learn how to hear from Him and how to communicate with Him. I encourage you all to begin by starting a journal. Ask God questions and listen to what He says in response by faith. Be patient. The answer may not come to you right away. And some are better at this than others. This will mark the beginning of an engaging dialogue between the two of you.

You can also do the same with Jesus. You can choose to talk to Jesus or God or both. Jesus is quite happy to speak to you, and He loves you dearly. But I encourage you all to develop this kind of intimacy with both Jesus and the Father, if you are able to do this.

Matthew has a book titled, *7 Keys to Intimacy with Jesus*[2]. If you follow those keys and put that book into practice, you will have no problem developing a rapport with Jesus. Matthew mentions his previous books for purely selfless reasons. He is not looking for additional sales; rather, he is looking to guide more and more people toward developing an intimate relationship with the Father and Jesus and has shared his expertise between the pages of his books.

I hope you've been encouraged by this message. I hope you choose to draw closer to God and Jesus. When you're finished reading this book, I highly encourage you to go and leave feedback and say which saint was your favorite. If it was me, then God bless you. I'll read it as Matthew reads these reviews from day to day. If he reads that you liked my interview, I'll be able to see that, as well. God bless you."

---

2.   *https://www.amazon.com/dp/B01LWU8U6G*

Visiting Eve in Heaven

As I was preparing my coffee, I received a vision of a house. I saw many tables and chairs, a coffee shop with snacks, as well as a full restaurant out back. Eve entertains people, and guests continually flow in and out of her house for amusement, entertainment, and fun. The tables and chairs are styled to match that of African culture, with unique designs printed on each one. The actual coffee dispenser has a tribal look to it. It looks like Adam and Eve came from African descent; that's what the décor of the place seems to be hinting at. I thought they were of Jewish descent, but it appears as though this is untrue, as the African details within the interior design of the home states otherwise.

I'm not familiar with African décor myself, so I can't really explain what I'm seeing, but I see a coffee shop with sweets, desserts, and pastries. It has a door out to a kitchen in the back where there is staff waiting to seat you and take your order.

There is a big-screen TV playing entertainment from Heaven there. People have individual headphones on each table. This is mainly for those who are enjoying lunch by themselves so they can wirelessly connect to the TV mounted on the wall and follow along with whatever channel is playing. People can also sit at the restaurant and talk to their neighbor, or the person they came with without being disturbed by the TV. The TV is there for those who want it. People can also put on a set of headphones and tune into live podcasts or different forms of entertainment in Heaven.

I know a couple of the saints in the first book did podcasts. I know the Apostle Paul had microphones on his desk and the other saint who was a music producer hosted a regular podcast, too. I guess you could tune into their podcast and watch them while you're at Eve's restaurant. The fact that Eve's house has a restaurant on its premises isn't entirely unheard of. In fact, it's quite a common thing to witness in Heaven. For instance, I know my house in Heaven has a café similar to Eve's.

"What do you do in Heaven?"

Eve answers, "I'm like a spiritual mother in Heaven, Matthew. People use me as their mentor. I mentor people in their faith, just like John and Paul mentor people and teach people the faith. I've developed a very close relationship with Jesus and the Father. I'm a lot like Rahab in that way; I'm very close to God. I have a great relationship with God, and I bring a sense of peace and a motherly perspective to my mentoring. I overshadow people with my faith, like a mother hen holding the chicks in her wings.

Many people who end up in Heaven had traumatic backgrounds. We heard a previous saint say that he works with people with trauma. I also work with people who just grew up in the church and didn't necessarily grow in their Christian faith. Some people become Christians and grow in their first year, and then they just live for another fifty years in the church, and they simply repeat the first year; they don't grow and develop in their Christian faith. Matthew's father was like that—he didn't grow a lot in his Christian faith. I take some of those people in and guide them through further learning.

These people also work with Jesus, and they meet with Jesus for routine conversations and assignments. I help them individually with their homework and counsel them. I have already learned nearly everything that Jesus teaches, so I have been promoted into a place where I'm a spiritual mother. I am the mother of the human race, and so I consider the children of the earth as virtually my own.

Heaven is full of personal growth. If you think you're going to Heaven and just go to the throne room and worship and not mature in your faith, you have a very limited view. Everyone who arrives here is first assessed to determine where they are in their spiritual walk. Then, they're given assignments and motivated to grow and develop intimacy and knowledge with Jesus, as well as wisdom from the Word of God. You may be wondering, *what else do we teach besides the Bible in Heaven?* Mary of Bethany said that there is no end to Jesus. Well, there is no end to the

Bible. The Bible has many layers of truth, and it's not really necessary that we use other books in Heaven to teach people the fundamentals of the Christian faith. The Bible is sufficient, but we do suggest other books for people to grow closer and more mature in their faith. There are many great authors on earth who have expanded on the prophets or on the books of the Apostle Paul. Paul and the other apostles have written their own books here in Heaven about their books and letters that are in the Bible.

For example, the Apostle Paul has written several books about his letters in the Bible. They're useful for people who want to study and dive deeper into the Word of God. By the way, Paul did not write them in the first year he arrived in Heaven but developed a much closer relationship with Jesus and the Father before he put pen to paper and recorded those books. And Paul keeps updating them as well. That being said, I prefer to teach from the Bible itself rather than from other source books, even those from the apostles like Paul. I consider the Bible to be sufficient to teach doctrine, for correction, and for living a proper life. If more people would read the Bible the world would be a better place.

I teach people by coming alongside and mentoring them. For example, people come to my restaurant and work on their homework that Jesus has assigned to them. They usually come with a friend. This enables me to sit with them and help them build their faith and be a part of the process.

Because of my important role, Jesus has given me the ability to speak to multiple people at once. Basically, this is similar to the way He is able to talk with millions of people at a time, but only on a smaller scale. For example, I can speak to my students in my mind, or telepathically, so to speak. So just as you speak to Jesus and He speaks back to you in the spirit, I can speak to my students back and forth without having to be face-to-face with them. By the way, you can do the same thing with the saints in Heaven. You can talk to them too. This is how this interview is being conducted. I'm simply speaking through Matthew, and you can learn how do the same thing if you want to.

I really love my job in Heaven, and there are so many people that are growing here. There are many spiritual mothers doing my job as well, and I appreciate my fellowship with them. From time to time, we have meetings in this room and the spiritual mothers and fathers come together. We have conferences with special speakers, and we learn from each other. If need be, this room can expand into a stadium, or we can go to one of the stadiums in Heaven and have that meeting."

"What do you like about Heaven?"

"I like the fact that you can learn anything in Heaven. If you see someone doing something and you'd like to try that, then you can. There's nothing stopping you. If you hear of something that you think would be exciting, you can pursue it. If you hear a speaker and you're attracted to what they're saying, their personality or their person, you can approach them, get to know them, and find out how they became that way.

Public speakers in Heaven are part of a community similar to the database of musicians and singers that was brought up in the previous book. The same is true for preachers. Through this network you can ask them questions and interact with them directly. For example, you could ask your favorite speaker, "What are the five most influential books that affected you about grace?" When they give you the list you can go and read them and then ask further questions. You just can't do these things on earth.

Another thing that has been mentioned previously is that time can expand in Heaven. You can spend what would be two hours of time in Heaven for a task, but actually take a week for you to get it all done. So a speaker has the time to answer hundreds of people's questions.

I enjoy the fact that you can become anything in Heaven. You can learn and be trained in anything, and you become exactly who you want to be. If you have always wanted to be a preacher, you'll have the opportunity in Heaven to preach. If you wanted to become a writer and you had the chance on earth, you can become a writer in Heaven. If you wanted to become a butcher, you could cut meat in Heaven and become a butcher. But the actual meat is formed out of light—everything is formed out of light. Light and frequency make up everything here. You can become a butcher in Heaven. You can become a chef in Heaven. You can become a mentor in Heaven. You can become someone who looks after children in Heaven. You can become whatever you want in Heaven. Whatever your desire is, you can pursue that in Heaven. And I especially love the fact that Heaven is a Godly place, so your desires become God-infused desires.

Of course, as other saints have mentioned, I love the idea of being able to meet so many people. I have those I work with on a regular basis, but I am still meeting people for the first time and love to chat with them. And the love in Heaven...It is so totally different from that on earth.

In the world there is money, time restraints, and pressure for people to earn an income to take care of themselves, their families, and those they love. These are all barriers to love. On earth people just don't have the time to sit around all day and talk. In Heaven there are no financial or time constraints so you to spend as much time as you please talking to people and really getting to know them on an intimate and personal level. In my line of work I speak to people, encourage them, mentor them, and coach them. But I also take the time to speak to others that I don't mentor.

On that same note, the love in Heaven is on another level because people aren't selfish. They're not trying to climb over each other. They're not trying to get to a position. There's no one-upmanship in Heaven. People don't study certain speakers, for example, so they can become better than them. There is none of that here. Sure, there is competition just as other saints have mentioned, but it's all selfless and for intrinsic purposes. There's no selfishness or envy in Heaven. So, with all the negative emotions taken out of the equation, it makes the love in Heaven a lot more sublime. The people here don't have any negative emotions whatsoever. And so, they love in a more wholesome way. It is truly a blessing to be loved in Heaven. The standard of love here between two strangers far exceeds your best friendships on earth.

Everything really comes back to taking money out of the equation. When money is taken out you can focus on Godly things rather than worldly things. It changes the whole game. That's the reason money isn't a medium of exchange in Heaven because God understands this principle and people are truly free."

"What is your message for us?"

"Earth can be a dark place when you consider people's sins and bad behaviors. So I encourage you to learn what Jesus taught and take the time to read Matthew's two books called the *Narrow Way: The Parables of Jesus Made Simple*[1], and the *Narrow Way: The Fifty Commandments of Jesus*[2]. Those books will help you learn and understand what Jesus taught, allow you to develop the mind of Christ, and allow you to love like Jesus. Love really is the most important thing. Like the Apostle John said ten times in his writings, "Love one another." Love is paramount. Wisdom and knowledge are empty without love.

The Apostle Paul stated that if you have all knowledge and wisdom but you do not have love, then it counts for nothing. So love is important, and I encourage you to learn how to love. Jesus explains this well in His fifty commandments, and Matthew does the same in his writings. Sometimes, he may feel a little embarrassed mentioning it so often, but it comes down to obeying what Jesus taught because being an authentic Christian is following in Jesus's footsteps.

Jesus said, "If you want to come after me, you must deny yourself, take up your cross, and follow me." In a life of self-denial, taking up your cross is crucifying your flesh each day and making decisions based

1. *https://www.amazon.com/dp/B08KHN14GD*

2. *https://www.amazon.com/dp/B08KTSYP57*

on what the Holy Spirit says to you. The fifty commandments of Jesus will help you make decisions based on what the Holy Spirit says. When facing a decision, you need to choose what the commandment says so you can follow Jesus properly. When you learn to follow Jesus, obey Him, and abide in His words, then you'll be truly free and holy. I encourage you to learn what Jesus taught and become one with Him. He says in John 17 that He wants His disciples to become one with Him. It's my wish that you would become one with Jesus and behave like Him. You must reach a point when you are faced with certain circumstances in life that you are able to behave and react like Jesus would. There's so much to learn and understand regarding what Jesus taught.

You're fortunate Matthew has already written books on this topic. He's put in the effort to share his knowledge with you so you can apply the wisdom in your life, allowing you to take on the characteristics of Jesus Himself. It's not so much the written Word that's important. It's the practice of the written Word that is crucial. You can have mental knowledge of the fifty commandments of Jesus, but without putting this into play with your whole heart, it is rendered meaningless. You can have knowledge that's born out of experience, and that's the type of knowledge that you need to possess. Not to sound repetitive, it's important to love. It's important to understand what Jesus taught.

I hope you enjoyed what I had to say. I hope you learn to love, and you learn to demonstrate the life of Jesus. If you loved what I had to say, please leave a comment on Amazon. God Bless."

Visiting Joshua in Heaven

First, I'll pray and dedicate this to the Lord. "Dear Father, I pray that you would be with us and give Joshua the right words to say, and that this chapter in the book will be encouraging to everyone. In Jesus's name I ask. Amen."

Right away, I see cattle. I see Joshua on a horse, and he has a hat on, looking like a cowboy, mustering cattle. He's leading them towards a milking pen. They're not beef cattle; they're dairy cows. He's collecting them all over the hills and leading them to get milked. On earth, milk cows make their way to the milk sheds by themselves. But for some reason, Joshua was out there riding and collecting them. This is part of his homestead. He has other young boys on horses, and they're collecting the cattle, too.

It's very interesting to see. He has up-to-date milking barns, and we can observe them leading cattle into stalls and putting suctions on them as the milk comes out of the pipes to be collected. I thought everything in Heaven would be different from earth, but this appears to be similar to milk sheds. Perhaps there's an unknown reason for why it exists here. We'll find out when we ask Joshua about what he does in Heaven. It seems that he's a farmer, but I have a feeling there's more to his role in Heaven.

Referring back to Joshua's house, he has a nice porch at the back. His house is three stories high and is made from wood paneling. It looks very nice and luxurious, and it appears to be a good homestead for him to live in. As you look around there are many cows and green grass for as far as the eye can see. He is taking me for a walk into his living room and there are paintings on the wall. If you approach the paintings, you can go to that part of the pasture on his homestead and visit with the cows and the pasture. All the cows are currently in the milking shed being milked.

It's a nice living room. There are wooden lounge chairs with wooden frames and mesh underneath, with comfortable pillows sitting on top.

Everything's made of wood in the house—wood paneling and beams. It looks like a farmhouse, although it's three stories high. The house also has a beautiful kitchen, and it seems that everyone in Heaven has walk-in fridges and pantries. Outside the door, there are also free-range chickens producing eggs on the grass. They have designated places to lay their eggs."

"What do you do in Heaven?"

"I'm a farmer, Matthew. I produce eggs and milk for other people in the community in Heaven. We have a good homestead here. We milk twice a day, in the morning and the evening. We have hundreds of cows; it's a big production. But my main job that I have here in Heaven is mentoring troubled youth, ages 16 to 20. I receive troubled youth that have come from earth from drug overdoses, speeding accidents, and suicides. I'm like a spiritual father to them. I have six to ten boys that work with me at a time. They all meet with Jesus once a week, like everybody else does in Heaven. But I disciple them and teach them the things of the Kingdom, and then they progress from my farm to another place and another situation. In earth time, I have them for a couple of years, and they undergo intensive training—kind of like rehab that you'd see on earth. These children had bad habits before arriving in Heaven, and here, we treat their trauma, and they are rehabilitated and set on a good path."

"Why have a good kitchen?"

"Some of them want to go and become apprentice chefs. They start cooking in my kitchen. I have a chef that works with us to train the young boys, and they take turns in the kitchen. A couple boys per day cook the lunches and dinners in the house. They're assisted by the chef, but they prepare lunch and dinner themselves. Some want to become chefs when they're older and undergo more intensive training by the chef during the first year of their apprenticeship. It may take them a year to realize that they want to become a chef. Then the next year, they enter their first year of apprenticeship.

Heaven is very much about sowing into people. Whether you know it or not, Jesus has a vested interest in our personal growth, and He wants to see us blossom into everything we are destined to be.

Some of these children will go off to work on other farms and become cowboys. Some of them may go off and do other things. Some of them become chefs. I've got one of my ten boys who's become a writer. He's been writing journals for years and has started his first non-fiction book. Matthew, you will be surprised that he's read all your books and has been inspired by you to write. He loves your books and he's been very interested in this series that you are doing. He's been tuning in and watching your YouTube videos. In fact, he watched as you edited the first book of the saints that you made from these videos. He's very interested in you and is like one of the great cloud of witnesses overlooking your life. He has a vested interest in you. His name is Jaymond. He's African American, and he's very interested in you and everything you have to say.

The farm is a wonderful place to spend time on. I have many people that come and visit us, as well as those from the Bible. After dinner, we have a Bible study and one of the boys leads a discussion from the Holy Scriptures. After we've finished the Bible study, a saint from the Bible will turn up and answer questions, thus making it an interactive Bible study. Imagine being part of a Bible study on the life of Joshua. Then, at the end of your Bible study, I turn up and answer your questions. The boys really enjoy the Bible studies because they know at the end of it the star of the story is going to show up and answer their questions. This makes them pay close attention so they can think of good questions to ask.

Heaven is just amazing. So much on earth is blocked out by our own minds, our own will, and our own emotions. Without knowing it we block so much of God out of our life. In Heaven there are no such filters. The soul of a person is not in control in Heaven—the spirit is. So much more gets accomplished in Heaven.

You could host or be part of a Bible study on earth, say studying the life of Daniel, and Daniel could turn up in a vision and talk to you. But you would have to have your spiritual eyes open to receive his message. Everyone in the group would have to have their spiritual eyes and ears open to be able to participate fully. Yes, it is possible. The same encounters we have in Heaven during our Bible studies could happen on earth. The difficult part would be finding people who can see such visions. Currently very few people on earth put in the time and effort to have such encounters.

I work as a farmer and as a cowboy, and we provide milk and eggs. We raise all sorts of animals, but we don't raise them for eating. We also have cats and dogs. Each of the boys has their own dog, and we lead a wonderful life here. My purpose is to sow love into these children and repair the brokenness that was in their life. You can be sure that I'm not the only one who does this. Every child that died an unfortunate death on earth is mentored and taught the right things. I counsel, help, and rehabilitate them into young adults that are responsible, happy, motivated, and have a full of life."

"What do you like about Heaven?"

"I like Heaven because you get to do what you're born to do. I led the Israelites into war, while also managing them alongside millions of people. It was a big responsibility. When I came to Heaven, I found my way mentoring trouble youth because I find that investing myself into ten boys turns those ten boys into leaders. I invest all my knowledge and wisdom into the ten boys that I have at a time. The group revolves periodically. I find that rather than spreading my time over a couple of million Israelites, spreading my time over ten boys is something that's very rewarding. And after our Bible studies I get to meet all the Biblical saints too. I get to fellowship with all the major saints in the Bible. We also study the lives of modern saints, like Bob Jones, Billy Graham, and John Paul Jackson, focusing specifically on their lives, their writings, and their teachings. They come to our Bible studies as well.

So, what I like most about Heaven is that you get to be who you're destined to be. Heaven is a place full of choices. You get to do what you want to do. There's no sin in Heaven, so you are able to always pick healthy options and follow your heart. I would've never known that I was destined to do what I am doing, but I may not do this forever. We have a system here where someone else could come and be the camp parent here and take my job, allowing me to venture into something else that may serve to be my calling at that time. I take time to speak, preach, and write books, as well. The young boy who is aspiring to be a writer, Jaymond, has read the books that I've written in Heaven. I may go on and do something else, but Heaven is a place of transition. You can go from one place to another. At present, I'm happy doing what I'm doing. I'm really enjoying pouring my life into these children. It's a great investment. I see them go on and be successful in their lives.

After they leave me, they come back and visit, and I visit them. In fact, I have established monthly check-ins with all the boys who've left my care, allowing me to keep tabs on them and ensuring they are following the teachings and guidance I've provided. They're forever going to be part of my heritage. I like that about Heaven. I love the people. I love the young boys that work with me.

I enjoy it when Jesus comes around to our house, speaks to the boys, and spends time with them. Of course, there are many stories in the Bible about Jesus, and there are many parables that we can cover in Jesus's life. I've used your book, Matthew, as the Bible study and then Jesus has come and explained it further, adding more detail and knowledge.

The boys saw Jesus 54 times, according to the 54 parables in your book. It was very enriching. We should record Jesus and give you the transcript of what Jesus says, too. That would make a good book.

Essentially, I want you to know that Heaven is all about choice, and Heaven is about becoming who you are meant to be. Heaven is about improving and drawing closer and closer to Jesus—becoming more aligned with who you were created to be. We get that in Heaven. We get to become who we're meant to be, and all our failures on earth are forgotten, making room for new successes to form."

"What is your message for us?"

"I encourage you to go over your favorite books. If you have books on Kindle that you've read and enjoyed, go over those books again with a highlighter and study them, incorporating the teachings into your daily life. So many people read books they enjoy, but they don't take anything from the book; they don't improve, nor do they implement that book into their life.

If you are reading this, then I encourage you to find your favorite books, perhaps some are from Matthew. Highlight them on Kindle or with a marker if you have paperback copies. Plan to implement them, write down things that you can change about your life, and start to make those changes. The Christian life is meant to be practiced; it's not meant just to be knowledge that remains in your mind. So many people in the Christian faith have the correct knowledge to the point where they can quote a verse directly from a book or the Bible, but they don't live out the Scripture, and don't serve as a testimony the words of Jesus. It's important to practice what you've learned.

Of course, Matthew has suggested several of his books that are crucial to put into practice as well, especially these two: *Narrow Way: The Parables of Jesus Made Simple*[1], and the *Narrow Way: The Fifty Commandments of Jesus*[2]. Understanding the teachings of Jesus is paramount to your relationship with Him, and your life as a Christian on earth.

You can start a blog and quote parts of the book and write down important points the writer brought out. Do whatever you can do to process the things you read. Perhaps you could start a YouTube channel, and start to quote parts of the book, and then give your explanation and commentary so others can benefit as well.

---

1.   *https://www.amazon.com/dp/B08KHN14GD*

2.   *https://www.amazon.com/dp/B08KTSYP57*

I really want to encourage you to become a better you—become a person who's effective and who understands the Kingdom of God. It's important that you listen to your teachers. But more importantly, apply what your teachers are saying. That's my encouragement for you. That's what I have to share with you. You have a reason. There's a reason why those books are your favorite books. If you go back to your favorite books, review them, and read them regularly until you are living what the books have got to say, then you will be successful in following the word of Jesus and living in your faith. I hope you are encouraged by this chapter of mine.

If you enjoyed this interview the most, write a comment on Amazon stating that you enjoyed what Joshua had to say. God bless."

Visiting Moses in Heaven

Let's start with what I can see directly in front of me. While preparing my coffee before sitting to write this all down, I saw Moses in one of his living rooms in his house. The living room was like the picture in book one of *Visiting Biblical Saints in Heaven*. It has two paintings, both about six to eight feet long, and six feet wide. The first image is a picture of God's hands, handing Moses the Ten Commandments on Mount Sinai. There is glory coming from a cloud, and Moses is fully lit up by this light. That was certainly a time that changed mankind. Moses broke the Ten Commandments the first time, and this is the second time he was given them. I really wish the world would obey the Ten Commandments and treasure them. I know that I've disobeyed the Ten Commandments myself, and I wish that the modern Christian world would still consider them as something worthwhile to follow.

The second image, which comes alive if you step close to it, is a picture of God in Heaven with Jesus, Peter, James, and John. I believe it was Peter, James, and John where God spoke from Heaven and said, "This is my son; listen to him." Peter wanted to build a tabernacle for God when Elijah and Moses were manifested on that mountain, as well. One of them came before they entered the promised land, Mount Sinai, where he got the law, and one was well after the promised land, when the nation of Israel lived in Israel. That was Moses visiting the promised land. They're both significant events in human history. When Moses went to get the Ten Commandments the first time, he came back glowing. When Jesus went up and Elijah and Moses were there, Jesus glowed, as well. Both paintings included the Father, and they were both amazing places.

Moses often visits with Jesus on earth through that portal. They've exchanged a lot of information through there since that day. They're powerful paintings to have in Moses' house.

The living room backs onto a fifty-meter swimming pool. He does laps and has people come over for visits. He has another place past the pool that resembles an auditorium or lecture hall.

"What do you do in Heaven?"

Moses answers, "I'm a spiritual father who oversees people in Heaven—more so a spiritual coach for leadership. I teach many of the upcoming leaders in Heaven. The fivefold ministry offices, apostle, prophet, evangelist, pastor, and teacher are earthly vocations. But there are people that come from earth that are going to assume our leadership positions in Heaven. I lecture those people, mentor them, and act as a spiritual father to them. They enjoy what I have to say. I've spent 2,000 years in the fellowship with Jesus and spent more than 2,000 years knowing God. I've developed a lot of understandable leadership skills since I led the people of Israel and have had the opportunity to apply those skills here in Heaven.

I'm pleased you heard from Joshua. He has assisted me in my lectures. He didn't mention this, but he deserves credit for aiding in coaching and mentoring the upcoming leaders here. True, he spends most of his time at the farm coaching those ten guys, but when he comes to the big stage, he mentors the leadership in Heaven.

You see, in Heaven no one is less, and no one is more. Even though there are leadership positions that not everyone can assume in Heaven, even some of the most mundane and regular people can speak and mentor others. There's a sense of equality running through Heaven. The people who are in leadership positions like me encourage people who are new to Heaven—even those that have been saved by the skin of their teeth and have barely made it into Heaven—to also speak up. It's our job to coach them, encourage them, and inspire them to grow.

Although I have a great deal of authority in Heaven, and I do exercise that authority, it doesn't mean I'm not a servant. It's the same with Jesus. He's the supreme authority in Heaven, but He's also kind to the children and everyone around Him. He's like everybody's servant. "Whoever wants to become great must become a servant of all," Jesus said. It's the job of leadership to serve.

While I enjoy mentoring the leadership of Heaven, I also enjoy dealing with the people who are growing in Heaven, and the people who barely made it here. When I bring a person who's new to the faith and I take them up on the mountain where God gave me the Ten Commandments, it blows their mind. When I take a person to the mountain where Elijah and I met with Jesus, it blows their mind. So, those portals are very useful for discipling people. They're powerful places to take people.

I have paintings all throughout my house. My house is a little like Mary Magdalene's, with pictures of Jesus hanging up everywhere. They're all living portals.

These pictures, or portals is you will, also serve as useful tools when mentoring others. For example, you can have a picture of Jesus preaching in Peter's boat to the people on the shoreline in Israel. You can take them through the portal to the actual scene and have them stand there for half an hour listening to what Jesus preached that day. This is also an opportunity for them to meet Jesus 2,000 years ago.

Heaven is so interactive. You can understand that those paintings become living portals that are full of instruction. If you ever wanted to go back in time and meet Jesus on earth, it's possible in Heaven. It's possible on earth, too. In fact, Matthew has gone back in time, met with Jesus, and spent time with Him 2,000 years ago. It all depends on whether you believe anything is possible.

The pleasure I have teaching the leadership of Heaven is amazing. The difference between the people I'm teaching now, and the children of Israel is that the people I'm teaching now aren't angry with God, nor do they complain about what God has given them. They all love God unconditionally and are all pressing on to fulfill their purposes in Heaven. They're all hungry to learn and listen and are prepared to do everything I suggest.

What I teach is aligned with what the Holy Spirit wants for them. It's not as though I'm their boss in Heaven. I lead them, but they're also led and directed by the Holy Spirit. It's a synergistic sort of relationship that we have. I offer talks and speeches in this lecture theater here in Heaven, providing each student with an opportunity to ask questions using their individual microphones. The lectures are recorded on video and are available to all leaders in here to watch. So, even if they're not at the actual lesson, they can tune in and learn, absorbing as much information as possible.

Nothing is wasted in Heaven. On earth, so many conferences take place that are packed with beneficial speakers, yet no one records them for those who are unable to attend. Well, these days most conferences are recorded, but there is usually a charge to watch them. It's all a money-making deal, and it is all rooted in external rewards. In Heaven everything is recorded so no one misses a thing. And there is no charge of course. It's a truly selfless endeavor."

"What do you like about Heaven?"

"I like the fact that you can be who you were created to be. I was born and destined to make a change in the world, so much so that the leader at the time had every baby killed because he was trying to get rid of me entirely. There was a sign in the stars, and I was felt in the demonic kingdom of something powerful coming forth. I was destined with leadership on my shoulders, and it suited me well to be trained in the Egyptian court. Like Joseph, I learned my leadership skills from the Egyptians.

I enjoy the fact that you can be yourself in Heaven. You can discover your gifts. It's a true joy to lead, direct, teach, and mentor people that are hungry for the truth. I get a lot of pleasure out of spending one-on-one time with others. I like having a meal with a person, one-on-one, at a restaurant or a café. I like asking people questions and getting to know them better. I like to take my students out individually to better understand their perspectives and personal characteristics.

Those I mentor are all tremendous leaders; but many of them don't have the authority and the anointing that my life has. Still, leadership is their destiny. They all hold leadership positions in Heaven. They all minister in Heaven in a powerful way. It's a joy to lead them.

Heaven is made up of rewards, where what you do on earth culminates in rewards in Heaven. That being said, Heaven has its own form of rewards. For example, I'm rewarded for the work that these leaders do. The content and knowledge I've embedded in their lives bears fruit, thus leaving me with multiple rewards. It's almost like one big pyramid scheme, where I get all the rewards from my downlines. I know Matthew finds that comment funny because he used to be in a multi-level marketing company, and that's exactly how it was with him.

However, in Heaven's scheme, Jesus is at the very top, and Jesus is the one who gets the most rewards. It says in Hebrews 12 that for the joy set before Him, He endured the cross, and we were the joy that was set before Him. Again, I'll have to say that the thing I like about Heaven the most is that you're able to be yourself."

"What is your message for us?"

"It's hard to speak after so many saints have spoken already and come out with something original, but I urge you to make your mark in the world, whether that's through the comments that you make on people's books, reviewing content online, or through word of mouth. That's one way you can really reward Christians. Good reviews bless writers, and some give hundreds of reviews, which helps guide and encourage others to read the book, as well. You could really make a mark on Amazon if you're a reader of many books and choose to leave a positive review.

It was mentioned previously that you should go back and read the books that impacted you and put them into practice in your life. You can start with those books. You can go back and read those books that impacted you, and then go to Amazon and write a review for each one, regardless of whether you bought the book on Amazon or not; you can still write a review.

Like the saints mentioned earlier, it's important that you name your favorite saints that have been interviewed thus far. This is just one way to leave a mark. You can also write your own books, assume a coaching position, lead a women's Bible study, complete flower arrangements for your church, or volunteer to clean the pews. There's so much you can choose to, and as long as it's selfless and kind; then you will succeed. Just be sure to make a mark. Do something that stands out and do something that shows the light of Christ coming through you to the world. Demonstrate Jesus with your life. Demonstrate Jesus with what you do in life and be sure to make a difference.

Matthew left so many reviews on Amazon that he became a Vine reviewer, which is a special sort of reviewer that is offered a special badge. However, after transitioning from the Amazon based in America to the one in Australia, he lost this badge. Regardless, as a writer, he understood how precious reviews were. At the end of each of these reviews, he always mentioned the 80 Christian books that he's written, urging readers to look at them and consider reading. He certainly has a few people following his reviews because they like to have a book recommended to them.

That's an easy thing you can do. You can really bless the writers by leaving reviews, but you can also bless the readers by doing this. You can spell out the things you liked about the book and why people should read it. Other people will be inspired to buy the book because of your review. Endeavor to make a mark on your life. And if you enjoyed this interview, write a review, and say that you liked Moses' interview the best. God bless."

Visiting Enoch in Heaven

Let's begin with a walk-through of Enoch's house. His house assumes an L shape, where all his living quarters are on one side, and all his entertainment corridors are on the other. There is a lecture hall that can seat 200 people, situated in its own wing of the house, alongside a restaurant that can seat 100. People visit the restaurant before and after attending lectures. At the top of the lecture theater, on the wall where the speaker assumes his position to deliver his speech, is a picture of people leaving earth to meet Jesus in the sky.

Enoch has a wonderfully big house, but his house is only one story. Normally, I see mansions in Heaven that are three stories high. Regardless, his house is spacious and luxurious. All the images hanging around the house are portals. He doesn't have a date on the rapture. There's no date on the wall stating when that's going to happen. But it's an exciting picture, nonetheless. When I was preparing for this interview, I was seeking the Lord for an image of the house, and I was shocked when I saw the picture of the rapture, knowing that it meant Enoch was going to have a role in the last days.

"What do you do in Heaven?"

Enoch says, "I'm a teacher, a mentor, and a leader of prophets in Heaven. I focus specifically on people here that were prophets on earth who are continuing in the prophetic journey, and even people who come to Heaven and train to be prophets for the first time. 1 Corinthians 13 states that prophecies will eventually cease, but it currently exists in Heaven. God is still speaking through His servants, and they're still having an effect in Heaven, while also influencing life on earth. Essentially, the Christian message should be infused with the message of Jesus. Jesus should be speaking through us often. We should be encouraging people with prophetic words, and the prophets do that in Heaven. They encourage people with prophetic words, speaking to their destinies and futures. The prophetic in Heaven is a lot purer, and no one misses the prophecies or gets them wrong because there's no flesh involved in the process here.

Bob Payne, Matthew's father, is training to be a prophet. In fact, he's one of my students. I teach and instruct prophets, running a school of the prophetic here in Heaven. For those reading these books who don't understand what a prophet is, let me set a clear definition before moving forward. A prophet is essentially a friend of God—a friend of Jesus. It is someone who knows the mind and heart of God. So in essence, everyone who is saved should be able to become a prophet. Everyone who's saved should be able to prophesy, speak on behalf of God, hear God speak, and pass messages onto other people.

I strongly believe the reason more prophetic utterances are not given in the Christian church is due to laziness. The prophetic is simple. It's listening to Jesus and His opinion, His message, and passing it onto others. Matthew was giving prophetic words before he knew what prophecy was. He was simply passing messages from Jesus onto people. He didn't even know what personal prophecy meant at the time, but he was doing it regardless. He was also a Baptist. He hadn't even been baptized in the Holy Spirit, yet he was prophesying.

If someone can do it without even knowing they're doing it, then surely someone can put in the work and effort and do the same. It all comes back to being able to hear Jesus and God speak. You can't prophesy if you can't hear God speak. I'd imagine that's the main blockage for people because a vast majority of Christians can't hear God. They only have the Bible for what God has said. They haven't received any testimony regarding messages God has sent them personally. That's why prophets are popular because people run to them to hear from God when they should be hearing from God themselves. Part of being a prophet is understanding the mind of God, understanding the emotions of God, speaking forth His mind, and speaking forth His will in the world and in Heaven.

There are many improvements that Heaven still needs to undergo. There are things that can be done better. For instance, the prophets can raise the level of worship, the prophets can raise the level of intercession, the prophets can raise the level of consecration in Heaven, and they can affect the temperature of Heaven. It's quite needful for me to mentor them and keep them aligned.

I was taken in my flesh body—I still have a flesh body in Heaven. I don't have a body like Jesus. But one day I'm going to return to earth as one of the two witnesses mentioned in Revelation 11 and I'm going to judge the world. That will be in the tribulation after the rapture. I'll be returning to a world that's very dark. And at that time, I'll have several prophets backing me up and walking with me on earth. They'll be in the spirit. They'll be walking with me and keeping me company, but they'll be walking from Heaven. In these last days, there will be many saints from Heaven coming to earth, working and walking with saints on earth, and applying and establishing the Kingdom on earth. It will be useful for you to open your spiritual senses and your abilities to speak to saints in Heaven because there are saints here that want to speak to you. There are saints that want to walk with you, mentor you, teach you, and instruct you. There are saints that want to be your friend. I for one want to encourage you and do mighty exploits with you.

Perhaps you haven't considered this possibility. Maybe you think that Matthew has these abilities to speak to us because he is someone special. If you don't have this gift, then the only reason is that you have not tried. Just ask Jesus because He opens this way up for everyone. If you are a Christian on earth, then you are seated in Heavenly places. All you have to do is open your eyes in Heaven, walk around, and start meeting us. We teach the prophetic books in the Bible. We teach the destiny of earth, and the destiny of Heaven. We teach people's destinies. We have prophets prophesy over each other in Heaven. And we record everything, so people can see and walk into their destinies.

I train prophets in Heaven, and I also train and encourage prophets on earth. Nancy Coen has met me, alongside Justin Abraham, and many others. They have spent time with me. I wish to meet a lot of people on earth, and hopefully people will see this book, open their eyes, open their ears, and invite me to come and spend time with them too."

"What do you like about Heaven?"

"I like that Heaven is entirely centered on Jesus. Jesus had such a pull—such an effect on earth—that he pulled Moses and Elijah down to meet Him. Jesus had such an effect on earth, so much so that the way we record time is based on Jesus's birth and resurrection. Jesus is the center of Heaven, and the people of Heaven worship Him. He's the King, and Heaven is His kingdom.

I like the way that the people of Heaven are made holy through their devotion to Jesus. I love how from the smallest child to the oldest person in Heaven—and some of us are thousands of years old—He remains the center and praise of all. Once you develop a hunger for the Word of God, once you develop hunger for Jesus, it becomes insatiable and continues to have you search for more and more wisdom, and more and more intimacy with Jesus.

Since Jesus is a good friend of mine, it does me good to see so many people worship Him, obey Him, and dedicate their whole lives to serving mankind and serving their fellow people in Heaven. The effect of their relationship with Jesus, and the effect of Heaven on people, makes people so loving. The love in Heaven is extraordinary. It can't be compared to the love on earth.

That being said, I enjoy meeting with any sort of person in Heaven. Sometimes people like Bob, Matthew's father, who wasn't too advanced or didn't focus much on their Christian faith are the most exciting to work with because when they become hungry, they *really* become hungry. Bob is really progressing well as a prophet. He's written two books since being in Heaven for two years, and he's working on his third as we speak. He's working on a book on the parables of Jesus as it applies to the people of Heaven.

Of course, the parables of Jesus apply for people who are still on earth, but for people in Heaven where no sin exists and love exists in a greater measure, these parables are interpreted very differently. Bob is working on Heaven's interpretation of these parables, while also collaborating with the Apostle Peter.

Heaven is a place where you can know the greatest of disciples, apostles, and prophets. Everyone knows everyone. That's another good thing I like about Heaven—everyone's relationships are rooted in others. What you learn from someone can be taken into your relationship with the next person, and what the next person has to say about that subject adds to what the person before said. Every relationship is beneficial, synchronistic, and works together—a good foundation that can be built upon.

Heaven is a great learning environment because people are hungry. People really get turned onto Jesus and turned onto the Kingdom. I really enjoy spending time with the Father and interacting with Him. And sometimes the Father will come into my lecture room and lecture the prophets. And He is also the guest speaker at times for a stadium gathering of prophets. That's a remarkable day. Imagine if you are called to the prophetic and are sitting in a conference with the Father and Jesus as the guest speakers."

"What is your message for us?"

"Get to know the Father—get to know God. You can find God in the Old Testament. If you read the book of Isaiah, you can really come to know the personality of God. If you read the gospels, you can really get to know Jesus. If you read the parables of Jesus and read Matthew's books on the parables of Jesus, you can gain an understanding of Jesus's teachings, and get a hold of what and who the Father is. Jesus said He is the expression of God—that He *is* God. And Jesus said, "If you've seen me, you've seen the Father." So, drawing on this statement, if you establish a concrete understanding of who Jesus is, then you also know who the Father is.

I encourage you to seek after the Father and get to know Him in a personal way because having a good relationship with Jesus is a good thing, but Jesus is just the firstborn Son, and God is amazing. God is every bit as loving as Jesus, and He as just as wise. But He has more authority and more anointing. Some would argue that it's not true—that Jesus and the Father have similar anointings. But I will leave that open for interpretation.

God is a wonderful Father to have. You'll find it incredibly beneficial and worthwhile if you learn to be prophetic and speak in the Father's voice. So many prophets tend to have an opinion that God is a harsh, judgmental, and vengeful God. They have a religious view of God, and they haven't had that religious sort of God tempered with the grace doctrine. But if you've established a foundation in grace, then God isn't as harsh and vengeful as you may think. You really need to understand God through the person of Jesus. I really encourage you to read about the prophets, get to know God, and read books that will help you with your understanding of God. I encourage you to do a search for books on God. Matthew has a series called *Conversations with God*[1] that contains four books in total. You can order this free on Amazon by searching for *Matthew Robert Payne*. If you read that series, then you can understand God's personality because you can hear Him speak about current situations and events.

I hope you've enjoyed what I've had to say. I hope you try to do what I say, get to know God, pursue God, and have a relationship with God. Every little thing you do before you get to Heaven will help you on your journey. In Heaven, it will help you to be elevated. It boils down to what classes you'll be eligible and suited for in Heaven. If you can do most of your work on earth to grow close to God and grow close to Jesus, you're going to enjoy your experience in Heaven a lot more. But even Bob

---

1.   https://www.amazon.com/dp/B01JN8X8GW

is having a good time, and he wasn't what Matthew would consider an advanced Christian.

If you loved my interview, be sure to post a review on Amazon and say that you enjoyed what Enoch had to say. God bless you and keep you."

Visiting Elijah in Heaven

I am receiving an image first of all the tennis courts on the premises. Then I see a swimming pool, and in the corner, a hot tub. It looks like Elijah likes playing outdoor tennis. His house is three stories high. I sense that in Heaven, everything is to be shared. It's not as though anyone plays tennis alone, but rather there's always someone to play against, or even to play doubles with. I see two courts and they are playing doubles on each court—eight people total. The spa looks like it would hold about twenty people, and the pool is twice the size. There are also tables and chairs for about forty people under an awning. Going further there is a commercial kitchen behind sliding doors. There aren't many houses on earth that have two tennis courts, a swimming pool, and a hot tub. And we haven't even seen the inside of the house yet.

"What do you do in Heaven?"

Elijah responds, "I mainly run prophetic councils, which are groups of people and leaders who meet to discuss, make declarations, and prophesy over the future of Heaven and earth. I often meet with prophets living on earth now that translate to Heaven for these meetings. Half the people on the prophetic councils are from earth and the other half are from Heaven. Matthew is aware of some of the saints on these councils that come here from earth for the meetings.

In fact, Matthew has a book where he was part of a council titled, *My Visits to the Galactic Council*[1]. I run those councils, and I sit on a number of them with Enoch in his lecture hall. I coach and teach prophets. I'm also heavily involved in the life of prophets. I'm going to join Enoch and visit earth to be one of the two witnesses mentioned in Revelation, Chapter 11. So, Enoch and I will come to judge the world.

I like my job. I like training and teaching prophetic people. I'm pleased to announce that I've spent some time with your father, Matthew, and he's very hungry for the Lord. Now he's very hungry for

---

1. *https://www.amazon.com/dp/B01N15J5XO*

the Kingdom. I've seen the first two chapters of his book on the parables. He's done a remarkable job, and your book on the parables really helped him through it.

What's beautiful about Heaven is there are no distractions regarding finances, jobs, incomes, bills, and worldly worries. People can be fully invested in learning about the Kingdom. If you are writing a book like Bob, then that becomes your full-time job. Bob is becoming a writer. You don't have to work in a restaurant in Heaven, be a florist, or be a butcher. You could be a writer, read books, and do research. That's exactly what Bob, Matthew's father, is doing. He's training to be a prophet, and he's becoming a writer.

What's especially wonderful about Heaven is investing in people. You invest your time in others and see the fruit of all your efforts. I also enjoy mentoring young prophets. I call them "young" because they've only been in Heaven for 20 to 30 years. I've been in Heaven for thousands. I enjoy mentoring the younger boys and girls. Please excuse us if we don't mention women that often; it's not by design. Of course, there are prophetesses involved in our groups, and we train many of them. Joshua trains 10 boys or so at a time. He doesn't train girls. This is largely because boys get easily distracted when girls are more present—even in Heaven.

Anyway, in our prophetic training we have many jobs and exercises to do. Some come up with prophetic words over the nations on earth. The Father releases those prophetic words through the prophets, and a prophet on earth speaks according to what he feels the Father has given him. But in reality, he is prophesying what a prophet in Heaven has already prophesied over that country.

It is assumed that the source of revelation for a prophet on earth is from the Father directly. But the real process works more like this. First the Father gives a prophetic word to a prophet in Heaven. That person speaks the word, and it is delivered to prophets on earth through the Holy Spirit.

Musicians in Heaven create songs and musicians on earth get their inspiration from them, without even knowing it. It's important to note that songs on earth are inspired from songs that have already been recorded in Heaven. Heaven interacts with earth more than people realize, and many prophecies on earth come from prophets in Heaven. In some of the prophetic councils, we release prophetic words to the prophets who visit from earth, and then the prophets speak them on earth. The prophetic is a powerful thing. It's a powerful source of information that can be used to lead, guide, and direct people to be who they are meant to be on earth."

"What do you like about Heaven?"

"I like the freedom of Heaven. I imagine that you can't fully realize what Heaven is like unless you've lived here. When you are living on earth with bills, constraints, salaries, tax, and inflation, you can't quite comprehend what life would be like if these things didn't exist. Even if the government is providing you with a paycheck, there's still pressure to pay bills, which inevitably causes stress. In Heaven, there's none of that stress. So, it creates tremendous freedom. Jesus said you can't serve two masters; either you'll love one and despise the other or despise one and love the other. He said you can't serve God and mammon at the same time. And so in Heaven, the other God, money, is taken away. There's no competition for God in Heaven. The whole of Heaven is focused on God. It's not focused on money. So, money's been totally stripped away, which creates freedom.

The people of the earth are in bondage to money. There's very little freedom there. Not only are people financially free in Heaven, but they're free to learn. They're free to chase down things that they're interested in. They're free to express their lives in any way they choose. They're free to pursue any vocation they want. There's no laziness in Heaven. Everyone in Heaven is contributing to the greater good. Everyone's role in Heaven impacts and helps others. I love the rewards in Heaven. I love the competition, too. I get rewarded for the fruit that my students bear—the fruit that comes from their lives. The fruit of their ministries reflects on me, and I receive rewards in Heaven for that. God is such a generous rewarder for people who place their trust in Him. Heaven is just the place for that.

Heaven is a place to really look forward to coming to. I'm pleased Matthew has decided to write this series of books because it provides a good description of what Heaven is like. If you read these books in the series—and there are a few more coming—you'll paint a good picture of what Heaven is like. Heaven has no limits. There are no hindrances. You can achieve anything you dream of. If you can dream it, you can achieve it.

Some people arrive in Heaven and have little faith. They've been beaten up with their image of God, and they've been angry at God. They've had a hard life and they've resented God for some time. They were bitter with God. When they arrive in Heaven, it takes a while to heal that bitterness and resentment. They have to come to know that God is a rewarder, that He is faithful, and that He is kind. They have to see God for who He is. Then they start to change and become hungry for the things of God. They seek out God and draw close to Him. That's when they start to dream.

First, they start with little dreams, like becoming a chef. And so, they become a chef. Then, they open their own restaurant, and their restaurant starts winning awards. Then, they may franchise their restaurant and have duplicates. Some of their other franchised restaurants start to win awards, and they grow slowly in their faith, believing they can do better and better as time goes on. The more they dream, the more they achieve.

Heaven is built for mankind. One day, there's going to be an earth like Heaven. There will be people living in nice houses at no expense. There will be no salaries. There will be no money. There will be a chance for you to learn anything you like. The more you hear about Heaven in these books, the more you can gain a better understanding of what the future earth will be like.

People have tried to emulate this on earth with Communism. Communism tries to create a Heaven on earth. But men are involved in this, and whenever men are involved, there's corruption. Unless Jesus is ruling on earth with an iron fist, it won't be possible. Heaven is a remarkable place.

I love the freedom that Heaven offers. I didn't live with much bondage in my life, but I certainly became scared with Jezebel's threat, and ran away. I wanted to die. I wanted to be taken home early, and God had mercy on me and did exactly that. But that just means I was given a second chapter to my life because when I finish my work on earth, I'll be overcome by the antichrist. But I'll achieve what I must achieve in those years. The earth will be scared of me.

In those days, like Enoch says, there will be hundreds of saints in Heaven traveling and working with us and with the saints on earth. Each of the saints will have mentors that they will be working with from Heaven. There will be a company of people on earth and a company of people from Heaven. So, you've got that to look forward to about what earth will be like in the future."

"What is your message for us?"

"Be true to yourself. You know what's right; you know what's best, and you understand what righteousness is. You understand what holiness is. Some of you struggle with sin. Some of you struggle with habits and ways of life that aren't pleasing to God. But through it all, still be true to yourself. Don't be a hypocrite. Don't profess Jesus and not believe in Him. Don't profess to be a believer in Jesus when you prove you don't believe. Don't walk away from your faith. Invest in yourself and in your faith. Learn what to do, how to live, and how to be true to yourself. Be genuine, be honest, be transparent, and let your light shine for others. Let people see Jesus in you. Let people experience Jesus in you. There's a way to develop the mind of Christ, and that is through understanding and practicing what Jesus taught.

There's a way that is true and right. There's a way that Jesus would approach every situation and behave under each circumstance. You want to reach a stage where you are behaving like Jesus. That means not gossiping, backbiting, or taking revenge on others. It means not praying for the downfall of those around you. Instead, it means praying for their wellbeing. You should instead bless your enemies. It's time to be true to your faith. It's time to be true to the discipline of being Christlike. It's time to destroy your flesh. It's time to put down the flesh and make decisions in the way that the Holy Spirit would want you to. It's time to learn how to walk in the Holy Spirit, and how to be directed by the Holy Spirit each day of your life.

It's time not to just be an ordinary Christian; it's time to walk just as Jesus walked. It's time for you not to be a Christian in name only, but to be a Christian in action. And it's time not to just read these books and say, "Well, that was a nice book." It's time to get your highlighter out and put into practice what's been taught. It's time to read all the books mentioned here and apply the teachings to your daily life. It's time to be real. It's time to wake up and smell the coffee. It's time for you to change. And Matthew speaks so much of this out of experience. That's why he's a good vehicle to deliver these messages because he's living what he's teaching. Someone had to make it possible. Someone had to live a life like Jesus. And you can, too. We encourage you to go after the books, read them, and apply them. It takes real effort on your part.

I hope you enjoyed my interview. Most of you will come home in the rapture and you won't see me on earth doing the job of the two witnesses. But you'll hear about it in Heaven. You'll see us doing our work from there. So, pray for your relatives, and pray for your friends that they may be counted worthy to go home in the rapture. God bless."

Visiting Mary, Jesus's Mother in Heaven

While looking in Mary's house, I see an image of her, not naked, but lying in a bathing suit against a wall. Down the wall is a cascading waterfall of warm water coming from a hot spring. The water is falling all the way down into a spa. She could lean against the wall and it would be like a waterfall falling on her. This is her bathroom. The water is always falling. There is a button that allows the roof to open and let the water fall through there, as well.

"What do you do in Heaven?"

Mary answers, "I'm highly revered by the Catholic faith, but not so much by Protestants. People in the Protestant church don't really respect me as highly as people in the Catholic church do. I'm just considered a normal person—a normal saint—by people in the Protestant church. They know that I was Jesus's mother, and they are somewhat happy to meet me, but not with much respect. However, Catholics confess that Jesus died on the cross for their sins. So, according to their belief, they're saved; they don't have to say a sinner's prayer to be saved.

I spend most of my time welcoming people into Heaven and helping them adjust—mainly Catholics. As you can imagine, there are thousands of people arriving each day. I don't have the time to meet all of them, but I make my way around and meet as many as I can, which is an honor.

Out of all the young girls in Israel, I was the only one who was chosen to be Jesus's mother. I was about 14 years of age when I became pregnant with Jesus. So, there was something special about me, don't you think? I uniquely trained Him up to be the Messiah. I did a good job of preparing Him for His earthly work. I was sad to see Him go. I have a unique perspective, and a lot of wisdom and understanding of Jesus's early life.

I would be a helpful saint for you to know. I possess a great deal of valuable information about the life of Jesus before He was in ministry. I even traveled with Him in His later years. Apart from that, I'm handy. I run classes in Heaven and teach people about the boy Jesus and what he was like as a child. I also discuss what He was like in ministry, and what He's like today.

People have a lot of questions about my life, and how I live. They have questions about Jesus that I am able to answer. I've developed grace and humility over the course of my life and can generally answer most people's questions about my Son. He's the Son of God, but He's also my Son. Yet, some people take exception to Catholics calling me the mother of God.

I was His mother; I understand Him well. I spend Sunday lunches with Him. If you consider a Heavenly week the same as an earthly week, I have a roast dinner with my Son and the disciples every Sunday.

So, everyone wants to meet me, but particularly people from Catholic persuasion. They want to meet me and have me bless them. And of course, I direct them to Jesus. Some people think that Catholics revere me over Jesus. However, once a person gets to Heaven, I steer their focus towards Jesus. I certainly don't encourage people to worship me. By the way, I *do* appear on earth in ways that are not demonic, as others have noted.

I have sat in on the prophetic councils that Elijah and Enoch host, and I've had a prophetic unction in my life. I like to speak to the women prophetesses, and I like to instruct the women in particular. I don't have a big position of leadership in Heaven. I'm not the queen, and I'm not treated like God's mother, either.

Matthew has a deep love for the Catholic Church. He's biased towards Catholics. For me, what's important is that people believe in my Son, and what's important is that my Son died for them. Everyone gets saved through the blood that my Son shed. It's not their belief in me that gets them into Heaven, but if their belief in me strengthens their faith in my Son, well, then that's a good thing."

"What do you like about Heaven?"

"I love that Jesus is the focus of Heaven. I love the idea that people love my Son. Now, I understand that Jesus was incarnated on earth, but before Jesus was born to me, He preexisted. Jesus is God—a holy entity. He's a lot more experienced than any of us humans. I understand that, but He's still my Son.

So many parts of His personality came from Him growing up, and He became the Son of man through becoming a man. And so, when I say that I'm pleased that the whole of Heaven worships my Son, I mean that as a mother. But I fully recognize that Jesus is an entity above me, and an entity that far exceeds me. I worship my own Son, as well. But it doesn't take away the pride in a mother's heart to see her Son recognized, and in the greatest place in Heaven. Jesus really is your answer. I love that Heaven is founded, directed, and centered on my Son.

I'm very much in love with the Father. He plays a big role in Heaven, and I enjoy worshipping Him. I call Him *Abba*, and I enjoy that He's given Heaven over to His son—for His son to be the center of Heaven. I enjoy His creation and that He continues to create things. Did you know that in Heaven, when an artist paints a landscape with trees and animals in it, the landscape is actually created by them painting that, and there's an actual tree that's planted, simply by the stroke of a paintbrush? And when that painting is hung, it creates a portal that can take you there.

I love the people of Heaven, too. I especially love interacting with people from all walks of life, people who barely made it into Heaven, and people with little or no reward in Heaven. I like meeting them and inspiring them to follow my Son.

I like meeting people who have done great exploits on earth, saved many souls, and completed great Kingdom endeavors. I love meeting bush pastors, bush missionaries, and other missionaries and evangelists from poor countries who have died through a crocodile attack crossing a river, or from a hippopotamus, lion, or other creature while traveling to share the Gospel. I love meeting the poor ministers of the Gospel. I love meeting the mighty ones from the West that have accomplished great things. I really enjoyed meeting Billy Graham face-to-face and thanking him for all the souls that he saved. He was pleased and happy to meet me and was pleasantly surprised when I took him out for lunch. We had a great chat. He dearly loves Jesus. Talking about Jesus was his favorite subject, and so, we had a great chat. He's been out for dinner with me, Jesus, and the disciples, and had a special time with us.

I love meeting people who've been in ministry. I love common Christians. I love Christians who are advanced and can talk to saints, Jesus, and angels, like Matthew. And I love meeting Christians who just sat in church and haven't grown so much, but still attended weekly meetings, like Bob, Matthew's father. I take people on tours of Heaven, but I mainly do my best work at cafés and restaurants just having face-to-face meetings with people.

I enjoy meeting with families and couples. It's not often that a whole family is in Heaven. It takes several years before a whole family is reunited in Heaven. However, every hundred or so years, a family is reunited, and I get to take them out for a family meeting. I can see where the seed of Jesus moves through the family, as well as the strengths and giftings in the families—how the ministry of Jesus has flowed through the family.

Sometimes you meet a great-grandfather that was a pastor, a grandfather that was a pastor, a father that was a pastor, and a son that was a pastor. It's great to see the heritage of Jesus passing through the generations."

"What's your message for us?"

"My message for you is to try and set a goal in life to develop the mind of Christ and have the ability to walk in the Spirit. Go after those two things with the intention that you want to develop the mind of Christ, to be able to think like Jesus, behave like Jesus, and to let the Holy Spirit lead you in everything that you do. For instance, Matthew started these chapters today by visiting Rahab in Heaven, and there are nine interviews that he needs to do for his second book. He started the first one thinking he'd just do a couple. Well, this is the sixth one that he's completed in a row. And the Holy Spirit told him an hour ago that he would be staying up all night to finish all nine interviews. This is a prime example of what walking in the Spirit is like.

Always set a goal to develop the mind of Christ, to have the ability to think like Jesus, behave like Jesus, and be directed all day long by the Holy Spirit toward worthy goals. Of course, you can work out what you're here for and do the Myers-Briggs analysis to determine your unique gifts and start walking in it. The way to develop the mind of Christ is to understand what Jesus taught. So, that would be found by reading and understanding the parables and commandments of Jesus. Obeying the commandments and letters in the Bible and taking every thought captive is how you'd learn to walk in the Spirit.

I hope you've enjoyed what I've had to say. And if you are leaving a review on Amazon, perhaps this may be your favorite interview, or one of your favorite interviews. If it is, please comment that this was your favorite. Tell the readers why they should buy the book and be encouraged. God bless you."

Visiting Joseph, Jesus's Father in Heaven

I'm seeing an image of a carpentry shed attached to a three-story house. I'm thinking of Mary in her spa bath as I observe Joseph's house. They love each other, but they're not living as a couple. This is a carpentry shed with all the modern equipment, like lathes and woodworking tools. It looks incredibly professional. In fact, it isn't just a shed; it is a whole factory located at the back of his house. There are all sorts of workers in there, building furniture and houses for those living in Heaven.

Joseph is there, and he's approaching me. He was just giving directions to someone else. As he walks towards me, he takes my arm and leads me inside his house. On the left-hand side coming in the back of his house is a wine rack enclosed in a glass room. Some of the bottles are 2,000 years old. Since you can go through these portals back to Jesus' time, you can get a barrel of wine from those days, bottle it, and bring it forth to today to drink and enjoy. Inside this wine cellar is a set of stairs that leads upwards. It's just one wine cellar, but it's three stories high.

Joseph has a commercial kitchen in his house, too. They all seem to have commercial kitchens. Like other saints, he has a dining table that fits 40 people. It's a large room and it's where Mary, the disciples, and Jesus meet with the family. He has a tremendously large kitchen—the largest one I've seen in Heaven so far. It would comfortably fit six chefs. There are a couple of chefs cooking in the kitchen right now. There are also all sorts of liquors and stuff in the house. There's a coffee machine and a couple of baristas in the kitchen, as well.

The dining room can easily be transformed into an entire restaurant. If they had weddings in Heaven, this would be the location to have it; it would easily fit 150 people. This would be a great place to have official functions and special events. If you were seated on the head table, you'd be considered an honored guest.

In the dining room that Joseph is showing us, there are people having a feast. The people eating are turning to face us. Jesus is in one of the seats, smiling at us. Mary Magdalene is there, alongside the disciples.

If you can picture this feast, then you can enter it and start conversing with all the guests there. Jesus is at the head of the table closest to the kitchen, and Mary's at the other end. Jesus, Mary, and the disciples are hosting a dinner for one of the families Mary mentioned earlier. This is a special family; it's the family that had the great-grandfather, the grandfather, the father, and the son as pastors. Those four men, and all their former wives and daughters and children are at the table. They're very happy to meet me and to meet us.

As you read this book, you'll come into this room, see them, and interact with them, especially if you're a pastor. It would be interesting to talk to the great-grandfather. In fact, you can say hello to him and have a discussion with him. He's sitting down now while the grandfather stands.

There are all sorts of pictures of Jesus's life hanging around the house, as well. There's one of Jesus as a little boy with some woodwork in His hands that He's made and given to His father and mother. Both Mary and Joseph are in the picture. He has a little cart that Joseph helped Him build. In the image, Jesus is about six years old, and He's giving the cart to Joseph.

This is a really good book for people who are experienced with translation because they can translate into these portal pictures and interact with Jesus. I've seen Jesus one time when He was a young child about that age where He was picked on by a bully who knocked Him over. I saw this vision and heard what His mother said to Him. It was helpful to watch and see how Jesus overcame this bully.

"What do you do in Heaven?"

Joseph says, "I'm currently working as a carpenter in Heaven. I was a carpenter on earth, too. Mary and I welcome people to Heaven. We put on banquets here, and there's a lot of wine that flows throughout, and a lot of alcohol that's consumed. This is not like the alcohol on earth and people don't get drunk in Heaven. There's no sin in Heaven. Alcohol is something that was created for our good and it's tasty here. People enjoy our parties. We entertain. Mary's house is more intimate, but we entertain here instead.

I build custom furniture for people's houses. I have a showroom in the city with all my designs and furniture. There, people can choose a table setting, lounge chairs, beds, or anything else, and we design it in our factory from scratch. There are many factories that I run, but this one is more specialized and is considered more high-end than the others.

I oversee a lot of carpentry, as well. Jesus will work in the factory and design furniture for people from time to time. Kat Kerr[1] mentions that people can get furniture with Jesus's initials on it, but Jesus still creates furniture in my factory. I think you'd appreciate a chair made by Jesus, but you'd appreciate having dinner with Jesus a little more than a chair.

I appreciate you coming to look at my factory and my house. It's not often that a person from earth gets a chance to tour the inside of my home. Perhaps you can describe it a little bit more, Matthew."

Matthew adds, "Well, the wine cellar is black, with black shelving and gold rims. The inside of the house is all made of carved cedar wood that looks beautiful, especially in dim lighting. The lights can be turned up and down with dimmer switches. As we walk into it, it's fairly dark inside. It gives off a good feeling. Jesus is telling jokes, and people at the table are laughing. We're just guests, but Jesus is the life of the party now."

Joseph continues, "I really enjoy making furniture for people, and I'm able to process special requests. People can come into our display shops and ask for a specific piece of furniture, and we'll take that special order for them. People know that they can get a piece of furniture from Jesus, and from time to time, we get an order for furniture from Jesus too. Jesus then receives that request and comes around to make it. So, that's what I do."

"What do you like about Heaven?"

"I like the fact that you can be comfortable doing what you do. I was a carpenter on earth, but it was hard. A lot of our clients didn't have much money, and so many people paid us in vegetables and goats. It was a difficult life. We weren't a rich family, and we spent all the gold that Jesus was given as a baby. We weren't wealthy. I also had a few children, which made it even harder to live. It's so much easier in Heaven with a house like this, and this is only the first story. Out back is an Olympic swimming pool with a spa and sauna. I have a couple of squash courts, that are located on the first level further down, and then there's another two stories above. So, I like that you can have the house of your dreams in Heaven. If you can think it, you can have it.

There's no selfishness or greed in Heaven either. People get what they desire because they desire it. They don't get it because they're greedy or they're selfish. Heaven doesn't tolerate sin. You can be sure that Heaven will accommodate you.

There are rewards in Heaven, and you'll be rewarded according to what you did on earth. In fact, what you did on earth will determine the first house you live in. Then, further rewards will enable you to acquire a bigger house, and so on. If you spent all your money on yourself, never gave to the poor, never financed your church, and were very selfish with your money while on earth, then you can't expect a house like this in Heaven. Not everyone in Heaven lives in a mansion. You have to understand that you've been visiting saints' houses in Heaven—Biblical saints that had a track record. I could take you to ordinary individuals' houses, and though some might be as expansive as those you've seen so far, they also might be fairly ordinary.

I like how you have freewill in Heaven. You get to decide what you want to do, how you want to spend your days, and what you want to do with your life.

I enjoy the people of Heaven. I love meeting the families that Mary gets to know, and when she has a family ready to meet the disciples and

Jesus, she brings them around and we have a good celebration. When the interview's finished, I'll be joining the table."

"What is your message for us?"

"Be authentic and be yourself. I know that's been said before by other saints, but it's important to find out who you are and be yourself. Don't try to be Matthew. Don't try to be someone you're not. Don't look at someone else and say you want a life like theirs. It's okay to want the gifts that they have, and it's a Godly desire to covet Godly gifts. The Apostle Paul said that we are to covet the gift of prophecy. The gifts of the Holy Spirit and the gifts of God are available for us to partake in. It's okay to want the gifts someone else has, but the only person you should want to be like is Jesus; the only person that you want to emulate is Jesus.

The Apostle Paul said, and we've said it so far in the books, "Imitate me as I imitate Christ." Imagine living a life so exemplary that you can say to people, "If you want to live the proper Christian life, just behave like me." Matthew has reached that stage in life, as well.

Be authentic and be true to yourself. Be honest with yourself, first. Find out who you are, who you're meant to be, and what you're meant to be doing, and do it. Start becoming who you are meant to be. I encourage you to do what the teachers are teaching you.

I really suggest you return to your favorite books, highlight excerpts that resonate with you, and ask questions. Get it down from your head, into your heart, and start applying it so you can live your best life. Start to become who you are destined to be. Matthew has a service called a Prophetic Destiny Blueprint. Order that service for yourself and have him describe what you're meant to be doing spiritually on earth. You can find this on Matthew's website.[2]

I hope you are encouraged by what I had to say today. I hope you got a good idea of my house and how I live my life here in Heaven. Perhaps you are a lover of wine and would like a three-story wine rack, too. Why don't you go to Matthew's website and go to the service to have your eyes spiritually opened[3], or go to the service of visiting Heaven[4] and come to my house for a tour one day? And if you're able to open your eyes spiritually, you can come to my house, meet me at the wine cellar, and we'll go upstairs together.

If you enjoyed this chapter of the book, you know what to do. Write a review on Amazon and say you enjoyed Joseph's interview. God bless."

Visiting Job in Heaven

I'm going to dive right into Job's house. I see a picture of a cinema that seats a hundred people. Job was known to suffer, and I feel that he invites people that have had a hard life around to his place—to the movies. There are movie cinemas in the main concourse of Heaven. But at this movie theater in particular, Job introduces the movie and delivers a speech afterward. He picks movies with a specific message and then gives his speech based on that. In other words, it's a ministry.

There's popcorn, chocolate ice cream, soda, and all sorts of stuff at the movie theater. The film can be a comedy, or a drama, but any movie he selects has a purpose and a message. Some churches on earth are run in theaters, but they don't show movies.

Outside of the movie theater is a coffee shop with coffee machines, pastries, and a kitchen out back. It has the capacity to seat approximately fifty people. The coffee shop also backs onto the Crystal Sea and has there's a second story that offers a balcony with the same view. If you travel further along, you'll see a fifty-meter pool.

"What do you do in Heaven?"

Job responds, "As you know, my story in the Bible is one that has motivated and encouraged many people throughout the ages. There are many who really suffered in life that have read my story and been encouraged. I like to speak to those people when they make it to Heaven. I establish groups, bring them to the movie theater, play a good film for them, and encourage them through a motivational speech. The theater is full twice a day with new people. The films are either earthly films or films made in Heaven. Either way, we have actors and actresses that star in those films here and are also able to chat with the audience afterward.

It's a multimedia presentation. We play the film and record the speech after. That means people can play a copy of it on their computers at home. They can broadcast it on their TV and watch the presentation. It's a powerful ministry, and I like to minister to all sorts of people. There are people in Heaven who've been here for a long time and have coped with their trauma. They're growing in their faith, and there are other messages that need to be reinforced in their lives. We can encourage them with another film and another speech. I very much love the medium of film, and I watched thousands of them throughout my time here. I conduct a lot of research by watching films. When I watch a film, I know what audience to bring in, and I formulate my message around this information.

I have a production studio in the house as well that I use to create clips of films and broadcast my speeches. I have a podcast that I host online too."

Matthew adds, "Job is using my house. I wondered why my house had been created, yet I wasn't there. This is where I film my videos. It's the third story of my house. The background on the zoom video is where my parents live. The second story is where this theater is. And it has a TV studio, radio recording studio, and a recording sound studio on the second story, as well. So, people come to the café and have something to eat. They go in and get served at the movie theater, have a soda, and watch a film. Then, they listen to a speech and maybe stop by the café on their way out. It seems that my house is being used to full capacity. I've often seen a couple of baristas at the barista station. I wondered why they were in my house. But a lot of people in Heaven come and hang out in my house. Job uses it."

Job continues, "I help increase people's faith, encourage people in their faith, and encourage their walk with God. And that's what I do in Heaven."

"What do you like about Heaven?"

"It's been said before, but I really enjoy the trajectory that people are on in Heaven. People arrive in Heaven with little knowledge, but their knowledge increases during their time here. Some people arrive lonely—from a place with no friends and a life of rejection. In Heaven, they find friends and feel loved until they're whole again. Some people arrive in Heaven having accomplished everything in ministry and being at the top of the world in ministry. Yet they find when they get to Heaven there are people who are a lot more advanced than they are, which humbles them.

And there are some who arrive in Heaven who got here by the skin of their teeth, like the Apostle Paul says. They just barely made it. Then, a spark is lit underneath them, and they are set on fire for Jesus, increasing in knowledge. So, I enjoy the trajectory that people are set on in Heaven.

It's also remarkable to see the wonderful work that the Holy Spirit achieves in people's lives here. The Holy Spirit is poured out on earth, but He designs and runs Heaven. And He really organizes Heaven in a lovely way. Everyone in Heaven is directed by the Holy Spirit, and their lives are ordered by Him. Whenever people submit to the Holy Spirit their life becomes full of freedom. It seems contradictory, but it is the way things work. You may think if you have control of your own life, then you'd be free. But you're only free by carrying out God's will in your life. The people in Heaven are more aligned to God's will than on earth.

I also enjoy meeting people. I'm somewhat of a hero in the wrong way in people's eyes. People want to meet me, and they know I suffered. There's a lot of wisdom in the book of Job. Not many people know that I was wealthy and used to be the equivalent to a government social security system in my city. I used to financially support the poor. I used to help people who were being taken advantage of. I used to rescue people from being abused. The elderly used to leave me their heritage and their inheritance. I was like a combination of a church and a government in my city before I was taken down. People don't understand that about me. Job Chapter 29 says what life was like before I got struck down, and we'll put that in the book right here for your reference, starting at verse 2:

2"I long for the years gone by
when God took care of me,

3when he lit up the way before me
and I walked safely through the darkness.

[4]When I was in my prime,
God's friendship was felt in my home.

[5]The Almighty was still with me,
and my children were around me.

[6]My steps were awash in cream,
and the rocks gushed olive oil for me.

[7]"Those were the days when I went to the city gate
and took my place among the honored leaders.

[8]The young stepped aside when they saw me,
and even the aged rose in respect at my coming.

[9]The princes stood in silence
and put their hands over their mouths.

[10]The highest officials of the city stood quietly,
holding their tongues in respect.

[11]"All who heard me praised me.
All who saw me spoke well of me.

[12]For I assisted the poor in their need
and the orphans who required help.

[13]I helped those without hope, and they blessed me.
And I caused the widows' hearts to sing for joy.

[14]Everything I did was honest.
Righteousness covered me like a robe,
and I wore justice like a turban.

[15]I served as eyes for the blind
and feet for the lame.

[16]I was a father to the poor
and assisted strangers who needed help.

[17]I broke the jaws of godless oppressors

and plucked their victims from their teeth.

¹⁸"I thought, 'Surely I will die surrounded by my family
after a long, good life.

¹⁹For I am like a tree whose roots reach the water,
whose branches are refreshed with the dew.

²⁰New honors are constantly bestowed on me,
and my strength is continually renewed.'

²¹Everyone listened to my advice.
They were silent as they waited for me to speak.

²²And after I spoke, they had nothing to add,
for my counsel satisfied them.

²³They longed for me to speak as people long for rain.
They drank my words like a refreshing spring rain.

²⁴When they were discouraged, I smiled at them.
My look of approval was precious to them.

²⁵Like a chief, I told them what to do.
I lived like a king among his troops
and comforted those who mourned."

Because of my great wealth and influence, I was not someone people would feel sorry for. And I was certainly one of the most righteous people that ever walked the earth. I have a real interest in people. I have got a real love for people. My suffering was born out of compassion, but I already had compassion for people before God allowed Satan to strike me down. There's a real lesson in the book of Job that Satan is on a leash. He can attack only by permission from God. Not everyone enjoys the book of Job. It contradicts their faith in some respects. Some people don't like to think that God could allow Satan to attack a person, but that's exactly what happened.

I really love how people can be set on a trajectory in Heaven going from the least and the last to the highest and the best. There are people that arrived in Heaven a couple of hundred years ago that are leading Heaven now. There are people who've arrived in Heaven, like Michael Jackson, who has won awards with his songs and competed with the thousands of other recording artists in Heaven.

There are people who've arrived in Heaven just last year who've written books and blessed people. Bob Payne, Matthew's father, is writing his third book, and he's only been up here a couple of years. He never knew he had it in him, but he wrote his first book about the history of Australians at war. That was a favorite subject of his while he was on the earth. He started off with his favorite subject, and then he moved on to a wider collection of prophecies that have been spoken over America. He collated many prophecies that were spoken over America and published it. The people of Heaven have come to understand what's going to happen in America. Now, he's in the middle of the third chapter of the book about the 54 parables of Jesus. He didn't know he had a gift of writing, but he's now working with Matthew's scribe angel, Bethany, and with the Apostle Peter.

Anything is possible. People can grow and be used effectively in Heaven. You could be a chef on earth and go straight into a job as a chef in Heaven when you arrive. Food is the same in Heaven; vegetables are the same. But all food is made from light. So, animals aren't killed. But as we previously mentioned in another book, fish are caught in boats with hooks, and they're released back. (Note that the hook does not harm the fish.) And so, Heaven is a wonderful place that allows people to reach their full potential, thus paving the way for healing. If you have had a hard and difficult life on earth, there will be more than enough years to heal your spirit and soul in Heaven.

You will reach a stage in Heaven where you are healthy, and you will be doing what you are destined to do. You will be completely happy about going to work each day. You will be learning about Jesus and growing closer to Him and God each day. You will go into worship, and enjoy it because your life will be healed. You will be fulfilled. You will have friends, family, and people around you that love you, support you, and encourage you. It sounds so different from Matthew's life on earth. And it sounds like such an exciting place to be.

As Matthew completes these books, he sort of finds himself pining for Heaven. I want to share with you that Matthew has three more books to go that he's planning on writing and publishing. He's planning on writing a book of nine musicians in Heaven. He's also planning on completing two books of nine people who are saints that have passed on to Heaven since Biblical times. And he will have two books of people that passed onto Heaven but weren't in the Bible.

There will be five books altogether for you to read. They will each provide an understanding of what the saint is doing in Heaven, an understanding of what the saint loves in Heaven, and a message from them for the people of earth."

"What is your message for us?"

"Please understand that suffering is only temporary, and you can be in extreme suffering, but still prosper. Matthew knows a couple of people that suffer in an extreme way. People with their condition have committed suicide before, yet they tend to hold on. Matthew is a bit of a weakling when it comes to pain, and he freely admits that. He can't understand how his friends hold on without committing suicide. Many people who have had a hard life commit suicide, and yet end up in Heaven. Much to people's disagreement, this is not a cardinal sin. It's not a sin that will divorce you from coming to Heaven, even though Catholics believe that is the case. They just keep people in torment who are already tormented souls.

I encourage you to look to the book of Job and to other people's testimonies who have also endured great suffering to find inspiration. You can find inspiration in Matthew's books. You can read Matthew's book, *His Redeeming Love*[1] for a history of Matthew's life up until eight

---

years ago. And you can see that he suffered and had a hard life filled with numerous trials.

One of the answers to suffering is reading books others have written about their own pain. You can be encouraged by reading through Job 29. And as you read that, you can read where I came from, and what I would've gone back to. And I was a type of a pre-incarnate Jesus. I was like Jesus Christ in the Old Testament. And I really enjoy my life here. I love giving to people. Heaven is all about giving, and your life should take on a similar form. Even if you can't do many things that were suggested by Matthew, even if you're just a reader of books posting positive reviews on Amazon, still give as much as you can.

When an author releases a new book, they usually won't have enough, or any, reviews. If you are one of the first people to review the book, your review will stay on the first page, and will get read for a long time. So, a good way to develop a bit of a name for yourself is to look out for authors' books as they become available, read them, and write a good review. That way, you can make a difference in people's lives. That's one simple way of giving that doesn't cost a thing. And even if your review is on the 30th page, it gives you practice in writing reviews, which is actually a real art form. You really encourage the writer by doing this and convince readers to give the book a chance. People can click on an option and see the latest reviews.

If you learn something at all from these books, write reviews on Amazon. If you got this book from Amazon, do Matthew a favor—and do the saints who spoke a favor—and vote for which saint you believe was the best to hear from. Write a review on Amazon and let that be the start of the reviews that you write for others. If you enjoyed what I had to say, write a review, and say that you liked what Job had to say. God bless."

I'd Love to Hear from You

One of the ways that you can bless me as a writer is by writing an honest and candid review of my book on Amazon where you purchased this book. I always read the reviews of my books, and I would love to hear what you have to say about this one.

Before I buy a book, I read the reviews first. You can make an informed decision about a book when you have read enough honest reviews from readers. One way to help me sell this book and to give me positive feedback is by writing a review for me. It doesn't cost you a thing but helps me and the future readers of this book enormously.

To read my blog, request a life-coaching session, request your own personal prophecy, or receive a personal message from your angel, you can also visit my website at http://personal-prophecy-today.com. All of the funds raised through my ministry website will go toward the books that I write and self-publish.

GET YOUR FREE BOOKS BY MATTHEW ROBERT PAYNE

To read more than 40 of Matthew Robert Payne's books for free please visit https://matthewrobertpayne.com.

Matthew also has 80 books in total on Amazon Kindle for 99 cents. You can find them here https://tinyurl.com/p69rch5x.

To write to me about this book or to share any other thoughts, please feel free to contact me at my personal email address at survivors.sanctuary@gmail.com.

You can also friend request me on Facebook at Matthew Robert Payne[1]. Please send me a message if we have no friends in common, as a lot of scammers now send me friend requests.

You can also do me a huge favor and share this book on Facebook as a recommended book to read. This will help me and other readers.

Please do not be afraid to contact me and connect with me. I enjoy speaking to my readers and all my best friends have read most of my

---

1. https://www.facebook.com/matthew.r.payne

books over time. I can't contact you as I don't know who you are, but you can contact me ☺

How to Sponsor a Book Project

If you have been blessed by this book, you might consider sponsoring a book for me. It normally costs me at least $1,200 to $1500 to produce each book that I write, depending on the length of the book.

If you seek the Holy Spirit about financing a book for me, I know that the Lord would be eternally grateful to you. Consider how much this book has blessed you, and then think of hundreds or even thousands of people who would be blessed by a book of mine. As you are probably aware, the vast majority of my e-books are 99 cents, which proves to you that book writing is indeed a ministry for me and not a money-making venture. I would be very happy if you supported me in this.

If you have any questions for me or if you want to know what projects I am currently working on that your money might finance, you can write to me at survivors.sanctuary@gmail.com and ask me for more information. I would be pleased to give you additional details about my projects. I currently have 5 books that I need funds to publish.

You can sow any amount to my ministry by simply sending me money via the PayPal link at this address: http://personal-prophecy-today.com/support-my-ministry[1].

You can be sure that your support, no matter the amount, will be used for the publishing of helpful Christian books for people to read.

GET YOUR FREE BOOKS BY MATTHEW ROBERT PAYNE

To read more than 40 of Matthew Robert Payne's books for free please visit https://matthewrobertpayne.com.

Matthew also has 80 books in total on Amazon Kindle for 99 cents. You can find them here https://tinyurl.com/p69rch5x.

---

1.   http://personal-prophecy-today.com/support-my-ministry/

About Matthew Robert Payne

Matthew Robert Payne, a teacher and prophet, enjoys writing what the Lord puts on his heart to share. He receives great pleasure from interacting with others on Facebook, hearing from people who have read his books, and prophesying over people's lives. He is a passionate lover of and disciple of Jesus Christ. He hopes that as you discover his books, you will intimately come to know Jesus, the Father, and Matthew through his transparent writing style.

Matthew grew up in a traditional Baptist church and gave his heart to Jesus Christ at the tender age of eight years old. But he left home at the age of eighteen, living a wild life for many years and engaging in bad habits and addictions. At twenty-seven, he was baptized in water and at the same time, baptized in the Holy Spirit. Matthew learned about the five-fold ministry offices and received a revelation of their value today.

He started his journey as a prophet twenty years ago, learning about this gift and putting it into practice. With thousands of prophecies under his belt, he can confidently prophesy to friends and strangers alike. He has been writing for a number of years and self-published his first book in 2011. Today he spends his time earning money to self-publish more books. He also produces many videos that you can view on YouTube.

You can connect with him on Facebook. You can sow into his book-writing ministry, read his blog, receive a message from your angel, or even receive your own nine-minute personal prophecy from Matthew at http://personal-prophecy-today.com.

GET YOUR FREE BOOKS BY MATTHEW ROBERT PAYNE

To read more than 40 of Matthew Robert Payne's books for free please visit https://matthewrobertpayne.com.

Matthew also has 80 books in total on Amazon Kindle for 99 cents. You can find them here https://tinyurl.com/p69rch5x.

Acknowledgments

I want to thank Jesus, the Holy Spirit, the Father, and my scribe angel Bethany for the knowledge and wisdom in this book. I want to thank all those above for the finances as well as people who support me in ministry.

I want to thank my friends Mary, Shayne, Dundy, Lisa and others who support me with their love. Your love is priceless to me, a broken man.

Last but not least, thanks to my readers who inspire me to write. I hope to do a whole series of interviews with saints in this format over the coming year.

[1] See https://www.katkerr.com. Last accessed Aug 5th, 2022.

[2] https://personal-prophecy-today.com/request-prophetic-blueprint.

[3] https://personal-prophecy-today.com/open-your-spiritual-eyes.

[4] https://personal-prophecy-today.com/visits-to-heaven.

Don't miss out!

Visit the website below and you can sign up to receive emails whenever Matthew Robert Payne publishes a new book. There's no charge and no obligation.

https://books2read.com/r/B-A-TLBC-WOLAC

BOOKS 2 READ

Connecting independent readers to independent writers.

About the Publisher

Accepting manuscripts in the most categories. We love to help people get their words available to the world.

Revival Waves of Glory focus is to provide more options to be published. We do traditional paperbacks, hardcovers, audio books and ebooks all over the world. A traditional royalty-based publisher that offers self-publishing options, Revival Waves provides a very author friendly and transparent publishing process, with President Bill Vincent involved in the full process of your book. Send us your manuscript and we will contact you as soon as possible.

Contact: Bill Vincent at rwgpublishing@yahoo.com

Lightning Source UK Ltd.
Milton Keynes UK
UKHW012302090223
416755UK00001B/129